THE SECRET LIFE OF
BIGFOOT

by Megan Cooley Peterson

Published by Capstone Press, an imprint of Capstone
1710 Roe Crest Drive, North Mankato, Minnesota 56003
capstonepub.com

Library of Congress Cataloging-in-Publication Data
Names: Peterson, Megan Cooley, author.
Title: The secret life of Bigfoot / by Megan Cooley Peterson.
Description: North Mankato, Minnesota : Capstone Press, an imprint of Capstone,
[2023] | Series: The secret lives of cryptids | Includes bibliographical references and
index. | Audience: Ages 9-11 | Audience: Grades 4-6 | Summary: "Think you know all
about Bigfoot? Think again! This apelike cryptid has a secret life that may surprise
you. Where does Bigfoot sleep? Does the furry beast have a massive stink? Uncover
these exciting facts and more through entertaining photos and easy-to-read text
that supports struggling readers and engages monster fans alike"— Provided by
publisher.
Identifiers: LCCN 2022041529 (print) | LCCN 2022041530 (ebook) | ISBN
9781669003939 (hardcover) | ISBN 9781669040378 (paperback) | ISBN
9781669003892 (pdf) | ISBN 9781669003915 (kindle edition)
Subjects: LCSH: Sasquatch—Juvenile literature.
Classification: LCC QL89.2.S2 P48 2023 (print) | LCC QL89.2.S2 (ebook) | DDC
001.944—dc23/eng/20220923
LC record available at https://lccn.loc.gov/2022041529
LC ebook record available at https://lccn.loc.gov/2022041530

Editorial Credits
Editor: Abby Huff; Designer: Heidi Thompson; Media Researcher: Jo Miller;
Production Specialist: Tori Abraham

Image Credits
Alamy: John Zada, 11, Steve Lillie, 23 (Yowie), The History Collection, 10, United
Archives GmbH, 13; Bridgeman Images: Look and Learn / Elgar Collection, 25;
Getty Images: Bettmann, 27, KLH49, 24, RichLegg, 29, yio, 20; Shutterstock:
Daniel Eskridge, 23 (Yeti), Dreamframer, 20, Giraphics, 15, guidopiano, 5, Ikrill, 7
(flashlight), JudeAnd, 19, Kenishirotie, 10 (lightbulb), Lifestyle Travel Photo, 12
(brush), Marina Zezelina, 14, Melody A, 28 (glasses), Savvapanf Photo, 12 (fur),
SFerdon, Cover (Bigfoot), Shad Selby, 9, simplevect, Cover, 1 (trees), 7, 28 (Bigfoot
silhouette), SlipFloat, footprint, 4, 7, 8, 10, 18, 26, 28, slowmotiongli, 17

Design Elements
Shutterstock: Kues, Net Vector

TABLE OF CONTENTS

Words in **bold** are in the glossary.

MEET BIGFOOT

What walks on two feet, loves trees, and smells bad? Bigfoot! It might be the world's most famous **cryptid**. Bigfoot characters have starred in movies and TV shows. Bigfoot even has its own theme park. But the hairy beast has a secret life you won't see on screen.

FACT
Cryptids are animals that may live in the wild. But there's no proof to say for sure. Some, like the giant squid, have turned out to be real.

BESTIES WITH BIGFOOT?

Think you know all about Bigfoot?
Can you name the cryptid's:

1. Height?

2. Home?

3. Biggest fear?

4. Name in Canada?

BONUS: Which U.S. president wrote

about a Bigfoot sighting?

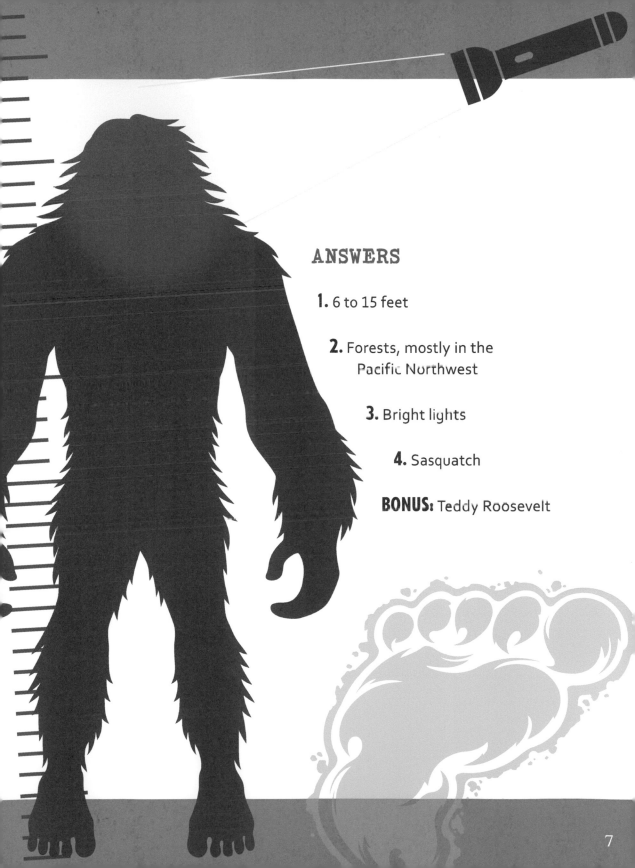

ANSWERS

1. 6 to 15 feet

2. Forests, mostly in the Pacific Northwest

3. Bright lights

4. Sasquatch

BONUS: Teddy Roosevelt

MY, WHAT BIG FEET YOU HAVE

It's a good thing Bigfoot doesn't wear shoes. No store has any big enough to fit! Bigfoot's hairy feet grow up to 24 inches long. Each foot has five toes. They look a lot like human feet. But way bigger!

FACT

In 1958, a California newspaper was the first to use the name Bigfoot.

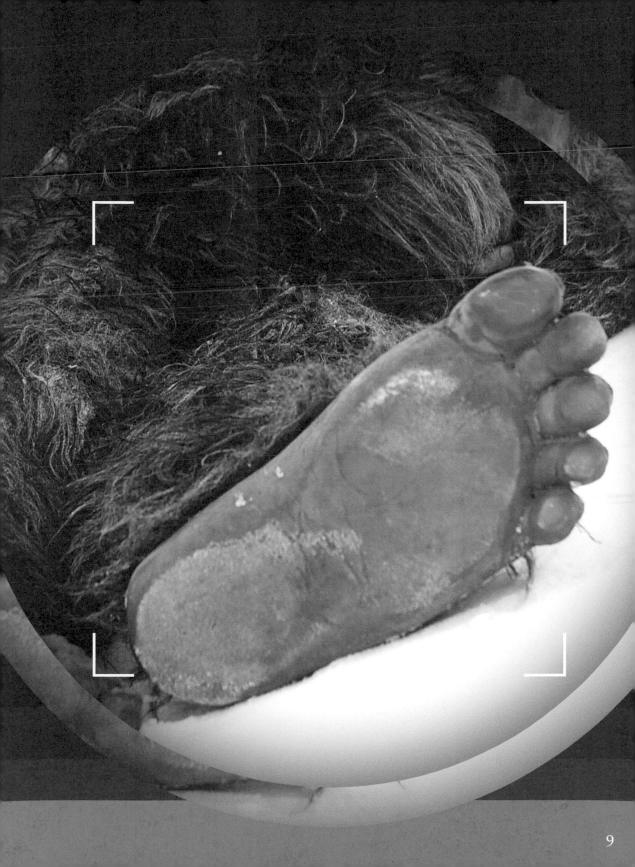

FIRST FOOTPRINTS

Bigfoot lived in secret until 1811. Then, **explorer** David Thompson found the first Bigfoot prints in Canada. They were 14 inches long. The prints showed sharp claws.

The prints were so strange. Something must be afoot!

Since then, Bigfoot fans have found hundreds of footprints. People make **casts** of them. It's almost like getting the cryptid's autograph.

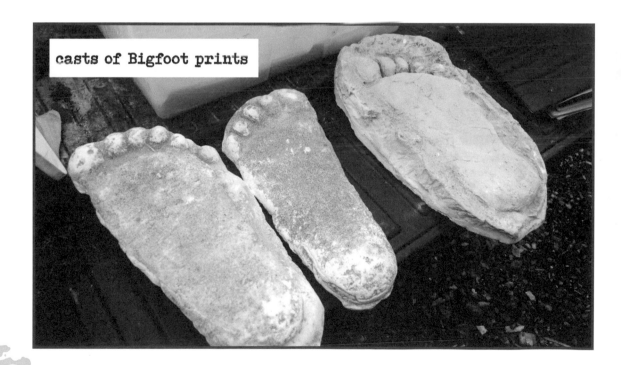

casts of Bigfoot prints

A STINK LIKE NO OTHER

What happens to furry feet that never get washed? They stink! Bigfoot's body has a gross smell. Some people say it smells like a dirty armpit.

In 1976, a man found what he thought was Bigfoot fur. The **FBI** tested it. Turns out, the hair was from a deer. Guess the man should have smelled the fur first!

HOME SWEET HOME

If you visit Canada or the northwestern United States, bring a camera. You might spot Bigfoot! This hairy **creature** lives in forests. The weather up north gets chilly. But Bigfoot doesn't need a jacket. Its thick fur keeps it warm.

BIGFOOT TOP TEN

These U.S. states have the most reported Bigfoot sightings in the world.

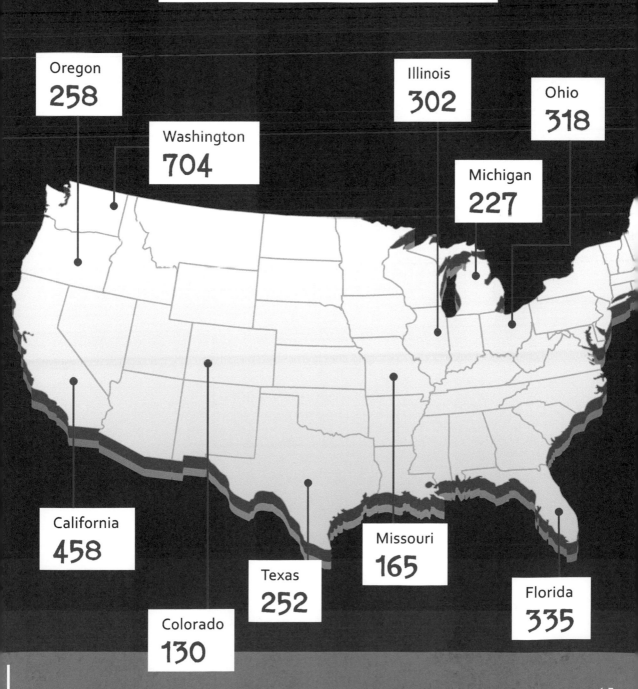

Oregon
258

Washington
704

Illinois
302

Ohio
318

Michigan
227

California
458

Texas
252

Colorado
130

Missouri
165

Florida
335

SWEET DREAMS

Where does Bigfoot rest its fuzzy head? Some people think it builds a nest to snooze in.

Many agree Bigfoot is a kind of **ape**. Other apes sleep in nests. They make them on the ground from twigs and leaves. Bigfoot might copy its ape friends when it's time for bed.

> ## FACT
> More than one Bigfoot are called Bigfeet.

a nest built by a gorilla, a kind of ape

⌈CAN WE TALK?⌋

Knock, knock. Who's there? Bigfoot! Bigfeet send messages to each other by knocking on trees and rocks. Think about that if you ever hear a knock in the forest!

These cryptids even have their own language. But they don't use words. Bigfeet growl, scream, and whistle instead.

SKREEEEE!

CAUGHT ON TAPE

A chatty Bigfoot was caught on tape in the 1970s. People took a mic into the Sierra Nevada mountains in California. They recorded grunts and howls. Some people believe it was Bigfoot talking. Or was it other animal noises?

FACT
The Sierra Sounds recordings are 90 minutes long.

THE BIGFOOT FAMILY

Bigfoot has family around the world. People have spotted other hairy, humanlike cryptids outside North America. Yetis live in chilly mountains in Asia. They have thick fur.

You can find Bigfoot family in warm places too. The Yowie lives in Australia. It has long arms and long hair. The furry Orang Pendek of Indonesia has a face like a human.

HAIRY MAN

Native people have **legends** of an animal that is a lot like Bigfoot. The Yokuts of California tell stories of Hairy Man.

This creature lives in the mountains. It walks on two legs and stands 8.5 feet tall. Are Hairy Man and Bigfoot the same?

This rock painting showing Hairy Man
is thought to be 500 to 1,000 years old.

LIGHTS, CAMERA, BIGFOOT?

Does Bigfoot want to be a movie star? Some say it already is! In 1967, Roger Patterson and Bob Gimlin were riding horses in a forest in California. They had their camera rolling. Suddenly, they spotted something. A hairy creature walked by. It looked at the camera. Was it Bigfoot?

The Patterson-Gimlin film became famous. People said it showed Bigfoot was real. Others said it showed a man in a costume. But no one has proven the film was faked.

Did the men find Bigfoot that day? Or is this cryptid still living a secret life?

GLOSSARY

ape (APE)—a large primate with no tail; gorillas, orangutans, and chimpanzees are kinds of apes

cast (KAST)—an object made by pouring soft material into a mold or other empty space, such as a footprint; the material then hardens so it can be taken out

creature (KREE-chur)—a strange animal

cryptid (KRYP-tid)—an animal that has not been proven to be real by science

explorer (ik-SPLOR-uhr)—a person who goes to an unknown place

FBI—a group that solves crimes; FBI stands for Federal Bureau of Investigation

legend (LEJ-uhnd)—a story passed down through the years that may or may not be entirely true

READ MORE

Cole, Bradley. *Bigfoot.* North Mankato, MN: Capstone Press, 2020.

Lombardo, Jennifer. *The Story of Bigfoot.* New York: Enslow Publishing, 2023.

Troupe, Thomas Kingsley. *How to Find Bigfoot.* Mankato, MN: Black Rabbit Books, 2023.

INTERNET SITES

American Museum of Natural History: Beyond Bigfoot
amnh.org/exhibitions/mythic-creatures/land/beyond-bigfoot

PBS: The Scientific Search for Bigfoot
pbs.org/video/the-scientific-search-for-bigfoot-dy3t8l/

Wonderopolis: Is There Any Proof that Bigfoot Is Real?
wonderopolis.org/wonder/is-there-any-proof-that-bigfoot-is-real

INDEX

ABOUT THE AUTHOR

Megan Cooley Peterson has been an avid reader and writer since she was a little girl. She has written nonfiction children's books about topics ranging from urban legends to gross animal facts. She lives in Minnesota with her husband, daughter, and cuddly kitty.